SELECTED

POEMS

BOOKS BY OSCAR WILLIAMS

BOOKS OF POEMS

The Golden Darkness
The Man Coming Toward You
That's All That Matters
Selected Poems
The Poems of Oscar Williams:
A record issued by Folkways

ANTHOLOGIES

The New Poems Series
The War Poets
A Little Treasury of Modern Poetry
A Little Treasury of Great Poetry
A Little Treasury of American Poetry
A Little Treasury of British Poetry
Immortal Poems of the English Language
Palgrave's *The Golden Treasury* (revised)
The Pocket Book of Modern Verse
The New Pocket Anthology of American Verse
The Silver Treasury of Light Verse
An Album of Modern Poetry
(issued by *The Library of Congress* and *Gryphon Records*)
The Mentor Book of Major American Poets
(co-editor with Edwin Honig)
The Mentor Book of Major British Poets
A Little Treasury of 20th Century Poetry
(three records issued by Colpix)

OSCAR WILLIAMS

SELECTED POEMS

OCTOBER HOUSE, INC. / *New York*

1964

Published by October House, Inc.
55 West 13th Street, New York

FOR GENE DERWOOD

CONTENTS

7

I SING AN OLD SONG

I sing an old song, bird on a charcoal bough,
Silver voice on the black black bough, singing,
Rolling heirloom eyes, burning holes in time,
Drenching the flank of nearness with drip-music:
The disturbed owner who hides everywhere
Lumbers through the miles of thick indignation:
The subconscious parts the nap-gold of afternoon.

I sing an old song, bird scything the silence,
Bundling sabres at the cornerstone of sense:
Bird, pulley on a hillheap of elves' eyelashes,
Silver piston sunk to a bud on the bough,
Sing, bird, sing, from the black black bough,
Shake the enormous atmosphere from your small fist
Of body, tear the colossal ear of the all around
Hanging loosely, like forest outside a window:
Open all the fluteholes of days until the world
Weeps music, and sweats light from every facet,
And tumbles to the smoking knees of its orbit.

I sing an old song, bead in the hair of the park,
Bird-knot in the weave of leaves, nugget in sieve
Straining gravel of Utopia to shining beginnings,
Deed, navel of matter, fleck of the future,
Knuckle knock on finality, sing, bird, sing:
Ride the groundswell of heartbreak, tap thick wrist
Of branch, lump of utterance in the cup of sunlight
Melt into the sweetness of reality, O:
Sprinkle effigies on the gauze of stillness,

11

Aim your gold beak from the nest, from the crook
Of the leafy black arm, towards the poised sun,
Swing girders from your beak through tin pretense
Into the underground room of man, the pallid palace.

I sing an old song, bird, toe-hold of song on bough,
Bundle in the bush of radiance: birth-cry of poem!

I THE MAN COMING TOWARD YOU

THE MAN COMING TOWARD YOU

The man coming toward you is falling forward on all fronts:
He has just come in from the summer hot box of circumstance,
His obedient arm pulls a ticket from the ticket machine,
A bell announced to the long tables his presence on the scene;
The room is crowded with Last Suppers and the air is angry;
The halleluiahs lift listless heads; the man is hungry.

He looks at the people, the rings of lights, the aisles, the chairs,
They mass and attack his eyes and they take him unawares,
But in a moment it is over and the immense hippopotamus cries
And swims away to safety in the vast past of his eyes;
The weeks recoil before the days, the years before the months;
The man is hungry and keeps moving forward on all fronts.

His hair is loosening, his teeth are at bay, he breathes fear,
His nails send futile tendrils into the belly of the atmosphere;
Every drop of his blood is hanging loose in the universe,
His children's faces everywhere bring down the college doors;
He is growing old on all fronts; his foes and his friends
Are bleeding behind invisible walls bedecked with dividends;

His wife is aging, and his skin puts on its anonymous gloves;
The man is helpless, surrounded by two billion hates and loves;
Look at him squirm inside his clothes, the harpies around his ears,
In just one minute his brothers will have aged four thousand years.
Who records his stupendous step on the delicate eardrum of Chance?
The man coming toward you is marching forward on all fronts.

RAILWAY STATION

Incoming train chattering opposite one's consciousness
With wheels moving restlessly inside the face of distance—
So the breath of the everyday expands through the station
Churning up a cloud of coffins above the advancing pistons.

Now the feet of the station are off the ground of Christian love,
The station is skipping rope with an elegant swish of arches:
A massive airiness, skirts blowing with a mass music of mind,
While the herd of backs, the trek from the subconscious, lurches.

Landing field of the strange strangers from the Mars of moment,
This is the land where the cat heads of the comets are buried:
The great clock of the nation peers from under the hood of history,
Like an eye staring amazed in the middle of the hostile forehead.

The ticket sellers are buried seated in the incandescent walls
But manage to meet the human race all gloved in travel dither:
Somewhere the long legs of highways stretch in torture under
The cavernous breach of landscape at the other end of the tether.

A canyonful of bells shivers to bits in a fit of innocence:
The railway station bends its head around the napes of silence:
Everywhere the shadows are budding on the tree of substance
Flowering into large leopards grounded swiftly on the pylons.

The train pulls in, tugging luminously at the leash of rails:
All the books are emptying their characters into the station:
The people who are quaintly decorating the mouthful of light
Reach for their hats and pasts and the luggage of frustration.

And the amazing direction called home branches everywhere,
Dizzying the dutiful compass and the compliant elements:
The attenuated female cry of struck iron bites at the wind,
And a powerful charge of flesh overloads the filaments.

This ant hill overrunning with nerves, with maggots of myth,
This tuft of winter lightning blooming in the cheek of travel,
This immense bulb wired in the bosom of a sullen universe,
This gathering of huddled veins—who shall unravel, unravel?

Who shall unravel this knot of light, the tangled sinews of man,
This kink composed of heroes and harpies, aims and omens?
For all the knots are Gordian knots until the mind is won,
The tyrant mind of the present unturned by the many poems. . . .

THE NEW SPHINX

The new sphinx with the lips of economics
Propounds the question, the gears grinding in the throat:
—What is reality?—and the man with the demon skin
Lets his amorphous eyes upward toward Paradise float.

And with wet seas of astonishment he now beholds
The insect glitterings of the amorphous sphere,
Huge foreign body trafficking in the blood stream,
Shrieking and disgorging the synthetic year.

From the back way, from the backyards of justification
Comes the question, its feet weighted with factories,
Sashweighted by the turbines, dynamos, dividends,
While the holy ghost of freedom cries among the trees.

The vandals are rebuilding the theatres again,
The crumpled curtains are smeared with imaginations:
The sequins are the glistering eyeballs of the men
Whose colossal virtue was their incredible patience.

The capacious demeanors of the gods are still unwilted,
The fields of molten corn come gliding from their hands:
The untiring sunsets have not yet—not yet succeeded
In designing an iron moment to cover the lands.

But the question hangs, a cloud frozen into chromium,
Frightening the pink-toed senses in their heated nest:
The sackcloth of martyrdom shines like a coat of mail,
And there are guns up the sleeve that sleep on the breast.

The radio, that angel's upper lip, repeats the question,
In the private air, in the closet mouldy with conscience:
The slough of the Sunday papers slaps at the windows:
Termites are living in the rotted music of the ancients.

The personal aggrandizement of earning a living
Prejudices the sincerity and the desire for an answer:
The sky fills the eye until it brims with the past,
And the search for reality grows keener and tenser:

And the opponent who disagrees remains the forerunner
Of that perilous matter, that element, the real:
And only when the drums stop to let the future pass
Does the man hear the small feet of the frightened ideal.

VISITING GENERATION

Gently but urgently exhaust valves are breathing now:
Eyes, full of light bulbs, roam in the overhead arches
Lighting up the dismal caked bones among the girders
And the frightened faces of buildings among the trees.

Stone lungs of history have difficulty in breathing:
The motor of silence is idling, idling, idling while
The brain cells are washing in the closed room of hush:
Inert knocker of human body slumbers on the vast door.

There's a bird in the girders laughing immensely,
Dropping the musical masks beribboned with rainbows:
The man below holding up the bowl of philosophy
Corrodes his fingers offering the bait of tea-time.

The bird checks in its orchestrations on the time clock
Sending time like lightning down the drain rod:
The man appeals to the police hiding out in the light
And gets very sick from having eaten too much god.

Who is this man with writhing swine for jowls, gorging
On the huge delicate cake fermented with the glass bones
Of heroes? He robs the borrowed planet, he breaks
Off silver architecture and topples it into the lake.

He strikes the match-head of sun, puffs the sodden clouds,
His shoulders sailing off upon a sea of barrel hoops:
He toasts his feet on the exuberant coals of music,
Gets up as the knock on the door empties the veins.

Sidelong, he coughs into the language of the ants and
Plays with the worm half over the fence of that realm:
He gazes fondly at the beast escaped from its clothes
Singing its dangerous doggerel at the rubberized helm.

The world sits in the mink coat of sleepless limelight
Picking tarantula headlines from the teeth of patience:
Metal emanations from the privy of evil
Assault the eye sockets of the visiting generation.

The stork flies through the mist with bullets for babes,
With blinker documents lest the blind blossom with eyes:
Though airplanes snore awake behind the back drop of events
Man already has reached an airpocket in the legend of mind.

TENT

Let us get up who drowse in the armchair of adage,
Who are outsnared by the eye of evening in the room:
The mask of heresy falls from the sanguine savage:
Outside flowers the populous body of the gloom.

The paws are crowding us out in our intimate tent,
The tri-humped fable, camel of horror, wants to get in:
The cold nose of the night steadily widens the rent
And pulls from our shoulders the ingrown annals of sin.

Better to unloose a flock of screams into the rain—
Swing open the door hung by the nerves over deeps of evil:
In the surcharged light there gleams the knob of the brain
On which lies hallucination, fingerprint of the devil.

Better to walk out with naked feet among the flawed events
Where unicorns stand toy-deep among crystal alps of jargon
And the rubber clouds leave in hordes the breathing vents
Jolted open by death rattles of the conjuring jaguar.

In the sandstorm of civilization's letters-of-the-print,
Even death is no shield—the tongue gets coated and wicked,
The lungs corrode and the springs are matted with lint,
And the girders crowd around the latest among the naked.

Obituary notices adorn the sedateness of daily features:
Somebody is committing the daily commonplace of dying—
Somebody barters a piecemeal past for a mess of futures—
Somebody is caught telling the truth, the headlines flying.

The oddest people die in the corners of our consciousness:
Lights, with half-names, go out, as in a harbor at night:
And death becomes a magnificent soliloquy in full dress
While we eavesdrop from the bottom of a shaft of light.

And from the bottom where we cower we hear the shoddy
Argument that reality gives to the anguish of the angel:
We are thrown like a hand grenade from the wrist of body
Among the boy demons romping in the celluloid manger.

Those who die die in a hurry, hand quicker than eye:
The details are pitiless that tell how the trick is done:
Meanwhile we button the day against the threatening sky—
Vast gold paw limping through mind, dread tread of sun.

Caught with nerve of the sweet tooth exposed to viewpoints,
Caught without clothing before the lustful emanation of ice,
We rip the weather strips of the last hour from the loins—
Our tent a sheet of newspaper, gesticulating flag of truce.

EDIFICE

When the eyelashes step gaily out of the wall of the skin
And bend over the wells of eyes splashing upward in the sun
Do they print a maze of black lace, palm wrinkles, maps therein
Upon the glazed look called sky igniting our yesterday's scene?

You who would search also under the overhanging bough of tomorrow
Find the golden furniture is wet and porous the silver façades:
Plush-colored haunches of time have cornered the foxlike marrow
Trembling in gaunt cloisters of bone in the shadow of the odds.

Our edifice of arteries bleeds windows full of light years
And fulfillment presents its face at the doorway of desire
Smirking, with gay hypocritical wig, with sweet tooth in arrears,
Stranger in friend's clothing, security's son, hireling and sire.

Let us break the mountain's venomous mushroom and examine inside,
And see the fresh black look of evil, gangrenous meat of vacuum,
Proclaiming that the flesh is a language the maggots use for guide
Through the thought-lit tunnels roaring into the millennium.

We must bite through the candy coating to reach the universe—
Plunge through the wound to reach the head on which change battens:
The raw inner lining is revealed when the momentum turns the curse
Face up, in the half light of Death's enormous blazing buttons.

Wall tall as brain—kingdom at hand—reality's body grows denser
Moving armies of unarmored flesh under the smoke screen of skins:
Superstition knocks at all the wood of the world but gets no answer,
While the meadow grows up on both sides of the lone and lonely fence.

23

Let us plant our feet on the platform of wind and drive forward
Or run naked down miles of disapproval under a chasing sun:
And face the barrage of dragon's teeth with temper grown froward
And angry and tall as a tornado's finger on the skyline of sin.

What happens to the garret windows of our values in floodtime
Or the droop-shoulder palaces under the heavy hand of the weather?
The stars are knee-naked, drunken, in the wine press of bloodtime,
And the ancient songs on the blasted landscape away must wither.

And baring its arms to the malevolent length of its pistons
The storm calculates the Augean problem as answerless-long:
Confusion is the sword that sleeps between knowledge and wisdom
And the cleansing rivers climb in at all the windows of our wrong.

DINNER GUEST

Evening, and the slender sugar tongs of a bird's small voice
Pick up the flawless square of our mood from the rim of thought:
We see the down on the big blond face of the Everywhere,
And the sudden flashing of the carnivorous smile of nature.

We are having dinner with the formal ogre of allness
At the Arts Club among the mirrors and paintings of mirrors:
It is breakwater moment and against a wall of grinning face
We perceive a radio, the last tooth posted within that mirth.

The cuckoo of light hops out, calling intimate time of the heart
Across the immaculate landscape of the tablecloth and the wine
Of realization, while the hands like gaunt animals are prowling
At the fable's edge, pecking at the crumbs of recrimination.

Dinner time, and the nervous system stretches its starved legs
Into the future, like a driven nail stretching out its length
Into a sea of wood; we are held by a hunger that is good for life;
And Tom Thumb is the guest of the ogre with the gracious mouth.

The famous paintings around us know how to stay adroitly dead
Giving off the soft lustre of the past and without blinking:
The dinner in the Arts Club flows on, a river of abstraction,
We are miles from the insane beggar who mumbled for a nickel.

What ever we die of, we shall never die of compassion
In a world lined to the browline with the bins of injustice;
Our fears leaven the bank balance to a frightening sum,
But the genial dinner ransoms the moment fallen among bandits.

We need no death's-head such as Egyptians had at their feasts,
The murdered circumstance stands with wet paws on the marble
Escaped from a movie of the future in the corner arcade;
Dining rooms grown dangerous in an age of guess and garble.

Though we soak our walls in music, patch the eye's blindspots
With murals of morals and dash about in a mess of mass,
We go through a lot of nature with our stupendous digestion
To reach the certainty of one noble sensation at the heart.

Ours is a last supper, without disciples; it is the atom supping
With the boulder, the bead of sweat with the cold great lake,
The eyeball's gloss with a planet on fire, the dot entertained
By encyclopedias of nonsense; man is the guest of the ogre mind.

AUDIENCE

The clock hangs to the walls by all its unseen fours
Edging closer along the sleeve of the audience:
The speaker pulls exhortations out of the doors—
Throws them to the virulent eyes in the wells of silence.

What is the man saying into the gullets of the many?
Now the loaves and the little fishes are divided in air
And fill the tossing foliage with a sound of money—
To a bushelful of birds' sound sticks the ring of despair.

The autonomous audience sits behind a brick row of brows
Mounted with the gun eyes, the doubts and the desires:
The hero medalled with solutions pulls out all the nows
And fans the sophistries forward, the sleeping ires.

The rows of children, too, with their townclock masks
Laugh an adult laugh or cough a grown up cough:
The teacher's awful stature dwindles between school desks:
Through a field of children's faces the future is off.

What if the audience rose from its buried victories
And smote the speaker with its wrath gloved in hill,
Would the word *revolution* fall out of all dictionaries
And leave in the speaker's vocabulary a growing hole?

What if the audience broke out of its boorish listening
And showed its bleeding ear, vast as a landscape,
And smashed the lead numerals on the world's fastenings
And sought through the entrails of its leaders for escape?

But this body bleeds long before the bullets reach it,
This stretch of nerves facing the depth-charge of drums:
And the underman of Calvin and the overman of Nietzsche
Burn in disintegration's glory in the auditoriums.

The huge child's-head of audience screams between girders:
Sleeping rivets of reality keep the beams flowing overhead:
And humanity bleeds through its open wounds, the leaders,
Its faucets of fire on the wall of darkness and the dead.

CAFETERIA AFTERNOON

I

In the cathedral vault with the great chromium gums
The girders of stifled laughter are now afloat:
The cafeteria opens its maw before a vast mirror
And a meadow's feet are disappearing down its throat.

Mushroomed with tables, this interior of history
Pours from the tall ceiling its palatial stair:
My mind tests a plank entering the century:
My hair explores the air-conditioned air.

This air smells of unemployment and chilled pallors
And people eating now in pairs and not in pairs:
The late comers on the frontier of no idea
Are sitting preponderantly upon their chairs.

The overlaundered old man lost in the corner
Has fallen upon the evil eye of his soup bowl
And is oblivious to the broad benevolent window
Where lies the summer sun, guttering ingot of gold.

My neighbor in front in the rustling coils of his paper
Leaps in a convulsive clinch with the leper of truth:
A snarling headline rises above his fat shoulders
And fastens into my panic its poisonous tooth.

The woman on my right is finished and getting up
In the distant mirror a league away in the room—
(Enormous female wrapped around the pillars of space,
You frighten me with the voraciousness of your womb!)

The man with the stag stare and the staggered teeth,
With the antlered thought above the frightened eyes,
Is marooned upon a coffee in the middle afternoon
Awaiting the three billion dollars from the skies.

In the streamlined rut behind the alp of counter
The moths with the human faces and in human clothes
Are piling into the furnace port holes of the future
Damp hunks of flesh, while the cold air softly snows.

Outside, the 'L' train angrily treads along the lintel
Shaking out a half skirt of desire through the door:
And Destiny who is both on land and on the sea
Stands cautiously revealed in this palace for the poor.

II

And while the national anthem maintains a flagstaff
Saluting the peeling of tickets from the tongues of bells,
Let us move with our mentholated preoccupation
Among the angel-eyed neons and the asphalt asphodels,

To commemorate the cloud descended from the tigers
And filed away behind the scrolls of a stone beard:
For the brigands are buying their bizarre supplies again
To hunt in the long-haired savannahs the little bird—

Now that the praying mantis of our time is amongst us
With subway kiosks climbing seaward out of its gaze
Peering at man peering back from the pit of his collar
And hanging fields of revulsion out on his aging days.

INDEPENDENCE DAY: 1939

The patriotic day explodes, and ten million hydra heads
Swarm from the decapitated headlines onto the beds
Of the frightfully awake who climb down into halls of heat
While the exhausted weather butters out the street.

The people standing silently at the curb are waiting for a bus:
Be careful, don't touch these people: this group is ominous:
If you look closely you'll see that they are not standing,
They are dancing, alive like lava, at time's ending.

The bus has just fallen on its studied rubber knees
And gulps these people through its national arteries:
It gets up with no neck broken or other defections
But casts haggard eyes, from both sides, in all directions.

Look further and you'll know it is riding an ocean of worms,
That the waves are self explosive and will not come to terms:
Though these people are on their way to the day after tomorrow,
They look over the edge to see from whom they can borrow—

They want to borrow the timber for a raft of faith on the deep
Where the baleful hydra heads make it seem appallingly steep,
Where the wind is full of slag, and the heydey fireworks leap
Over the nation fitfully turning in its frightful sleep.

CAMOUFLAGE

The brain sitting like a spider within the web of the hair
Resolves its two bright eyeballs in the lunar and solar glooms,
And the keen hunger of that gaze whistles through the air
Cutting the warm large worm of nature into millions of rooms.

The planet is a mountainheap of magical bird's-eye views:
Death drives a mind behind each leaf and buds are eyes on boughs:
The land is gasping for breath, the soil bubbles with mouths:
The landscape at all the windows is raping the great manhouse.

Who is this army moving behind knots of trees, shapes of air,
Spreading decades of slime on the pristine maps of the future?
The quicksilver needle of sex gleams behind the rushes of hair,
The clothing of the day shows traces of the weeping of nature.

Those are no bodies of angels ascending the eardrum of the sky,
Only the broad back of humanity climbing the subway stairs,
Only the wall-wide shoulders of the commonplace that cries
Hunting for music boxes among the steel beams of the nightmares.

We see that the skin is poured like a waterfall down gaunt bone,
And the wolf's skeleton agitating within the body of the lamb:
We see the plight of the smug man in his edifice of self alone
And that an agile sin has escaped the net works, the sin of sham.

Camouflage skysilvers the eyeballs with the callousness of youth,
Hypocrisy pours germs in the fissures of the falling-apart brain:
But all things represent each other so as not to miss the truth
Should it saunter in among the mile-tall palings of the rain.

An ailing race of women and a brawling brotherhood of men—
We snare the radium-haired animal by its renegade nerve,
With the whorls on our palms untraveled orbits, our fingers ten,
To find our image a sample sail on the blackboard of make-believe.

No need now to paint the ship's gunwales so they melt into waves
Nor draw the tidelines on the walls so they look like stairs,
Nor sew on the coat of the coward the brocade of the brave—
The feet of Death are standing among the shapely legs of chairs.

And the hanging gardens of time are tethered at our necks,
And sex is a brushful of paint, a loin cloth deceiving nobody:
The pounding of continents on the window of the sea is terrific
While we coddle the past with our fashionable quilts grown shoddy.

The factions of men are steps to that sea, the giants' causeway,
Where deeds once walked and time quavered into beds of stone:
And it's neither—neuter—nether, with the age upon the pauseway
Looking through the open windows of the Stonehenge of our time.

O velvet voice of the fictions! O fractures of fixations!
O hound with the long tongue of money bleating at the real!
O radio like an animal nibbling the inside ear of the nations!—
These are death's-heads of the subconscious at the feast of the ideal!

Who is to tear these miles of sheet iron from the wound of history
Or destroy the embroidered wolfcoat around the nakedness of song?
The deed lies in the image and its gristle-beak of mystery
Taps in the skull, and it won't be long now, it won't be long. . . .

THE LEG IN THE SUBWAY

When I saw the woman's leg on the floor of the subway train,
Protrude beyond the panel (while her body overflowed my mind's eye),
When I saw the pink stocking, black shoe, curve bulging with warmth,
The delicate etching of the hair behind the flesh-colored gauze,
When I saw the ankle of Mrs. Nobody going nowhere for a token,
When I saw this foot motionless on the moving motionless floor,
My mind caught on a nail of a distant star, I was wrenched out
Of the reality of the subway ride, I hung in a socket of distance:
And this is what I saw:

The long tongue of the earth's speed was licking the leg,
Upward and under and around went the long tongue of speed:
It was made of a flesh invisible, it dripped the saliva of miles:
It drank moment, lit shivers of insecurity in niches between bones:
It was full of eyes, it stopped licking to look at the passengers:
It was as alive as a worm, and busier than anybody in the train:

It spoke saying: To whom does this leg belong? Is it a bonus leg
For the rush hour? Is it a forgotten leg? Among the many
Myriads of legs did an extra leg fall in from the Out There?
O Woman, sliced off bodily by the line of the panel, shall I roll
Your leg into the abdominal nothing, among the digestive teeth?
Or shall I fit it with the pillars that hold up the headlines?
But nobody spoke, though all the faces were talking silently,
As the train zoomed, a zipper closing up swiftly the seam of time.

Alas, said the long tongue of the speed of the earth quite faintly,
What is one to do with an incorrigible leg that will not melt—
But everybody stopped to listen to the train vomiting cauldrons

34

Of silence, while somebody's jolted-out afterthought trickled down
The blazing shirt-front solid with light bulbs, and just then
The planetary approach of the next station exploded atoms of light,
And when the train stopped, the leg had grown a surprising mate,
And the long tongue had slipped hurriedly out through a window:

I perceived through the hole left by the nail of the star in my mind
How civilization was as dark as a wood and dimensional with things
And how birds dipped in chromium sang in the crevices of our deeds.

SUBWAY

Under the church's lawn, in the land of electric clocks,
The subway train is plunging into the lungs of the rocks:
And as the bald Negro with the glasses reads his *True Story*
And the old woman is quivering behind her morning glory
The inconceivable girl with the timetable, feather and leer,
A mammoth dumpling of sex, is ensconced on the atmosphere.

Beneath the tons of complacence the subway deftly delves
With people sitting satisfied with their incomparable selves:
A child across the way is dangling out of a fairy tale book
Dipping in the advertisements the divining rod of her look:
The dismal fans are languidly stroking the beard of the wind:
Behind the newspaper fronts the sins of thought are sinned.

This is the skin of death and every pore is a face
Pulsating against tomorrow, the vacuum thighs of space:
This is life the story teller, telling endless tales
To keep himself alive as the iron eyelid falls:
This is the explosion chamber, the secret room of the spark
Where the populations whirl with the poured breath of the dark.

A jungle of prongs is scraping the tough hide of the present:
The huge centipede of station leaps at the vein imprisoned:
The subway's galvanized throat is torn into craters of speed:
The sullen meantime is bulging with the ingots of greed:
And what is true is in conspiracy with the thing that seems
And steel continues to scream, so long as man screams.

DWARF OF DISINTEGRATION

I

Who is it runs through the many-storied mansion of myth
With the exaggerated child's-head among pillars and palings,
Holding in his grip the balloons of innumerable windows
And chased by the flowing malevolent army of the ceilings?

It is the dwarf, the yellow dwarf, with the minted cheeks,
With the roots of the fingers, with the wafer-thin cry,
In the maze of walls, lost in the nurseries of definition,
While shadows dance on shins of trumpets in a waning sky.

Voices are wired in the walls and rats are gnawing rumors,
The throat of music is bursting with the leadpipes of lust,
And the giant's face on the dwarf's shoulders is frightened
As the battle sounds strike the panes from the near-by past.

The pillars in the palace are reclining about like pistons
And the horses of parenthesis have run away into the woods:
The king is caught on the vast flypaper of the people:
There are holes as big as hovels in the wall of platitude.

The queen is ill from planting the garden with progeny
And her eyes are crossed off by vicious marks from her face:
She telephones the dwarf who puts his head in the instrument
To find his features come out in glacial coal bins of space.

The orgasms of distant guns attack at the lustful curtains
And soldiers are standing about in historical knots of lies
Warming the frozen tag-ends of lives around the spontaneous
Combustion of bosses who are stoking hollows of hired eyes.

The swine bulge in the snake bellies of the telegraph wires
And bellow under flat clouds of ceilings in the interior;
Communication swallows the quicksilver swords of distance;
Headlines perform, in squadrons of plumes, on the warriors.

But the draughty palace of fable is full of feeble splendor,
And the yellow dwarf now in possession of knowing documents
Runs after the newspapers cackling on the edge of freedom
While the golden cupboards tremble for the aging sentiments.

The music of battlefields exhilarates the hidden overhead
And injects into the air a breakdown sense of release,
And the numerals wriggle off the lock boxes of the world
Unloosing a swarm of the venomous vultures of the peace.

But the dwarf, the yellow dwarf, with the sunspots for eyes
Is hunting in the archives in the moth holes in the palace,
And he tightens the torture boot around the spinal column,
The steel twilight gleaming with the sweat of his malice.

II

Now that the battle is on, keep off the palace grounds,
You can hear the dwarf rummaging in the elephant inside:
It's better to draw a curtain of birds around your eyes,
Or fall into the picture book under the thumb of a landslide—

Than to come upon spiders eating the iris of the eyeball,
Or glimpse the yellow dwarf digesting the members of princes,
Or see famous paintings loll, like tongues, from their frames
Into a roomful of heroes pretending to harass pretenses.

38

The sagging structure is propped between thought and thinker
The gilded lawns flow on under the smokescreen of the laws:
The allover attack of a decaying body infiltrates to the atom,
Even the beast in the violin hangs out with lopped-off paws.

So run into the first thicket of verbs, the nest of deeds,
Place a skyline between yourself and the grandiose emblem,
For the inquisition wears the hypocritical jowls of a palace,
There's nothing here to salvage, and yours is another problem.

39

AUTOBIOGRAPHICAL NOTE

When I crawled out of the padded pit of the commonplace
And poked my head into the giants' land, the rarefied air,
I realized time was thick with adults like the familiar face
That was sitting back into the hollow palm of a motorcar.

I saw he was the man with the diseased hands hidden in gloves
Who wrote advertising to while away the split-second decade:
He said through a sifting voice, 'I have been theorizing now
For ten years, and there's nothing I can do but lean on my record.'

I looked into my notebook for the house numerals of my actions,
But in it I found only the telephone number of a dead woman,
And while I was standing perplexed, voiceless among the fictions,
A creditor whistled that I come down from my birds'-eye-view pronoun.

But evasively my eyes put on the felt slippers of frustration
And I stole through the giants' land on seven-league tiptoe:
I heard God howling from all the music boxes of the nation,
While the private dynamos spat out public headlines, with photos.

I said, I must take it easy, the surface here wears golden teeth,
The landscape kisses the feet, but trapdoors lie under the roses,
The beam in my eye is likely to fall like a thunderclap of brimstone:
So I went to the young man who was massive and looked like Moses.

But the bulky young man had a tenacious unsatisfactory wife,
Wrote vast trilogies on America, fell voluminously in love,
And committed incredible suicide by hanging in a hotel room in Reno:
Civilization roared on, into the darkness of the nervous system.

I ran to the worker with the one ear, in the first frost of events,
Who was applying the blow torch of mind to the callus of reality:
The radio spluttered platitudes in glittering chips on the lens,
'Forgive me,' he said, 'but do you hear a big sound under the sea?'

I went to a man whose passion was buying libraries from the insolvent,
He was hiding out in his skin, the arsenal of all the factions:
He said, 'Do you know of anybody—' I said, no, all the poetry books
Are lying like nightlights in the homes concerned with major issues.

I attended an evening reading given by a mogul of mediocrity
Who has read his poem about a whale for twenty intolerable years:
The lights were dim, the room half empty, the great world snored,
And busses tumbled from its nerve-ends to the heartbeat of the spheres.

I said, all bad things come to an end, even the answer mongers,
Every day has its dog, and lo, around the corner lies an immense day:
What do I know of poetry among so many definitions?
This undoubtedly is life, and there isn't a soul that wants it that way.

II JEREMIADS

JEREMIAD: I

Beside the steering wheel we stand,
The latest favorites of time:
The elder heroes melt to land
Where spars of newer skylines climb.

The gold tooth of the lovely morn
Deep in the candy of the age
Is surely one that cannot scorn
Our scientific heritage.

We are the hope of decades past,
The gilt-edged dream the dreamers dreamed:
We nail a cannon to the mast,
And in a cloudburst it shall gleam.

Our agile airs, the movies spry,
The beats and bugs, that bite our youth,
Attack the vistas of our sky,
Like swarming locusts of the truth.

Rumors of fear that crop the brain,
Discouraged hands that knead the heart
Precipitate into a rain
Of fire and foulness on our art.

The band is wailing on the air
—Darling, I am growing old—
The atmosphere gets dark with hair
And sluggard shoulders of our gold.

44

Voluminous with unswung bell,
The fable of the daily bread
Blooms forth its dear perennial
In the fat gardens of the dead.

The dollar slaps the broad back of
The mighty minute of each day:
The marriage look betrays the love,
Below the deck the hipbones play.

Our century is dressed in streets
With milestones mildly making haste:
The radios from ringside seats
Look triple-eyed and double-faced:

And baby-eyed and bargain-faced
The promise leaps the printed page:
There is no safety from bad taste
And scarcely any from the age.

LAZARUS

What is it that they leave undone
The men who died who do not die?
Huge thumb of blood, the sunken sun
Presses the earth through wells of sky.

The elder boulder falling back
Reveals the eyrie of the night:
Battalions tumble from that crack
With human faces strapped on tight.

Two billion heads of Lazarus
Into the changeless daylight stare:
The myrmidons grown ominous
Pull at enormous flags of air.

The squadrons bend their knives of doubt
On whitened statues to the poor:
And blackened hillsides stand about
At windows in man's furniture:

While in the storm of bursting years
The blue wood sunders with great sound:
The bright undriven nails of stars
In dreadful clusters slap the ground.

O all is open, insecure,
Shot with the doorways of dark myth:
There falls at thresholds of the pure
The massive elbow of man's death:

The massive elbow falls across
A snowy landscape, thunderless:
Two billion foreheads sway and toss
That slept in caves of nothingness.

Two billion soldiers leave the grave,
The snake-skin of their martyrdoms:
And music's blessing makes them brave
Through resurrections loud with drums.

Valkyrie headlines tear the brain
And shriek above the hills of men:
And surely they have died in vain
Who do not want to live again!

THE DREAM

In a dream I saw civilization fallen,
A city lay collapsed upon a plain:
The debris was piled upon the fields
Like a thick paint upon a bad painting.

My companions and I were not concerned,
We lay idly on our backs and we talked
Casually around the campfire of the mind:
And then it was that a woman walked by:

Tigers were her eyes on the landscape
And they tore up our thinking like paper:
But we pretended we were unconcerned,
And covered our hearts with the talk of the day:

That life was casual, the world was usual,
The small things good, the good things small:
That another day's work was finished, finished,
The city lay collapsed, civilization fallen.

WHY THE SEA IS SALT

We are affrighted now to think: we fear
That noise, the people, in the wind-washed bushes;
Our endless childhood has a cavernous ear;
It is no rainfall splashing quoits—that's clear!—
It is a sound within the house we hear—
The headline breaks, and out a nation gushes.

And bugles' clouds like giant mushrooms blow
Along the golden airways down the mind:
Out of our house oblivion's billions flow—
The mills of the gods grind slowly, but not so
The appalling world upon the radio
Pouring its iron tides upon mankind.

And now, now, the machine now cannot stop
Exploding brimstone on the music's stair:
The earth is filling, filling to the top,
No room now for the cyclops in the shop
Nor elsewhere at the gargoyle curtain-drop
Of faces headlong on the final air.

49

JEREMIAD: V

When the bird flew from the Columbus hull
And swung our canyons from its fabled beak,
Or gravitation donned long gloves of bough
To drop its apple in perception's lap,
How was the embattled Spirit to conceive
Monstrosities lay breathing in the good,
That limbs of lambs could grow the heads of wolves?
The multitudes who built a wall of graves
Around the golden calf of nothingness
And faced the deathrays of the deathless smile
Through the vast stretches of injustice brought
The flower brimming in the crack of light—
They open valves to brimstone on our sleep
And freight our air with tons of memory.

Now out of reservoirs of misery
Our language glistens with a flow of tears
And history sweats its worms out of the books;
While prodded by war planes of an angry day
Out of abstraction's bed we turn to meet
The gigantic sense of failure darkening
The many windowed framework of the skull.
And once again, and maybe more than once
Again, must we put down the clockwheel tools
And apron of our carelessness, and rise
And throw our bodies, our bags of blood, against
The rocks of Mammonhood and so blot out
The evil writing on the tidal wall,
The Red Sea running down the heart of God.

MAN, FRIGHTENING ANIMAL

Man, frightening animal, snarls in the chains of gravitation,
With godhead, a quicksilver skeleton, in his body,
The miracle of language hanging from his tongue;
He crawls down the boulder of history, gleaming and bloody,
Drinks from the well, the æons panting from his lung,
And anoints his forehead with the starlight of elation.

Man, tinkering with his gewgaw civilizations,
The fragrance of music raging around his bone,
His heart a sea of paws and a roar of despair
Drags the huge evening out where he stands alone,
Terrifies the ants and dismays the solar air,
While the beaks of skylines sink in the flesh of nations.

His propellers are peering at peaks that scatter
In the darkened bosom of the moth and the morning year
Above guttering seas whose light no wind can put out:
Man drinks of the deep and his eyes become clear,
Dissolving the telescoped walls of his death and doubt,
For this is the way of his faith and the mastery of matter.

The walls are levelled to terraces of splendor,
While melted are the many mirrors of the enemy
To blue lakes of peace humming songs of light and bread,
And the air is cleansed of the shoulders of antiquity,
Cleansed of the debris of the inconsiderate dead,
And the canyons overrun with the morning's crescendo. . . .

INVISIBLE MENDING

Now watch the sick man in the hospital
Clawing at the nurse's inner eyes,
His past is crushing him in the bed
And he is groaning like an engine;
But invisible mending follows the deathbed
Floating on the crest of a skyscraper,
The fates open newer spools lustrous
As the absolute eyes of an angel.

Go visit in the prisons the men
With the sheet-iron faces of tomcats,
Who kept the face of justice open
By putting a foot in the museum's door;
These are the men who dropped petitions
In the wringer of law and fled
With jackpots clanging like fire-alarms
In the top floor of their conscience.

Or go sit with the stony hypocrites
Come in from the shadows of the newspapers,
The sieve of hat passed around
Disintegrates the audience like a tiger;
And while the organ rolls on its tongue
The coated canyons of acquaintance
The daylight of peace is pouring
Through the stained glass on the foundations.

Or be shot from the cannon of the circus
Aureoled in the rare of mathematics,

Float up with the performer above
The foreheads in amusement's laughing areas—
You will find yourself in a vast mist
Of puppet-strings hanging from airplanes—
A rain of wires, the strafing lines
Catching the audience in its seat.

And yes, you are inside the catacombs
Humming with the weaving escalators,
Inside the structure with the cellar
Windows at which horizons drink like deer,
Lost in a hymn of iron stairs
Floating down from fate's doll-like eyelashes,
A race of toy saviours sailing
On conveyor belts out of the mind.

It is a nest of telescoped boxes,
Painted humpty-dumpties hiding in each other,
But the tree in the seed in the fruit
In the flower sways from the pivot's point,
And you find beneath the focus,
The end not final, is crinkling with answers,
That invisible mending begins to wrinkle
Beneath the deepest bite of the bomb.

THE MAN IN THAT AIRPLANE

The man in that airplane once lay in the womb
He flies like a lark in a place full of room
In the clouds to get a good look at his tomb

The man in that airplane once clung to the dark
His shadow is strewn over meadow and park
Where God airs the light the man seeks his mark

The man in that airplane once curled in his mother
Where he couldn't move to get at his brother
Now he flies straight in the face of his Father

OBITUARY PAGE IN WARTIME

As I arise like Samson in the mist of falling walls
Into the upper strata of forty years I hear
Great sounds, the waters of the world eating away
The immeasurable ever-deepening groove of time.

I hear also the skull-grenades out of the endless
Cup of the loins, the faces on the obituary page,
That hung unexploded on the century's bald air
Break into the bright of death, the noiseless light.

All were friends, I knew of their names, knew
That they devoted lifetimes to their public lives,
But shattered thus against the invisible at last
They spill down, minor fireworks in an age on fire.

Authority on turf, the Expert on horses for fifty years
Falls, and on a day stampeded by the world's values;
On the same day the Mexican Envoy; and the noted Chemist
Follows leaving a trail of four wives and properties.

The Insurance Head of the international corporation,
The Secretary of the seaside company, makers of foam,
The Lawyer from Atlantic City, all were in a hurry;
None of these could wait till the end of the story.

Now I hear the bells of an undernourished Christendom
Huddling in their niches and the voices that run
Down the rumorous veins of the aggregate conscience;
The mourning takes place behind private mountains.

I look through the bright cross cut into the door
And watch the mighty nightsky, the storm of stones;
The church is still entrenched among the living ones,
The acrobatic traffic is crossing swords of horns.

The harbor whistles, tall fountains, arch the mind
As the city pours itself quickly around the survivors:
The heart facing heavily into its dénouement, asks
What is the sum of all these extraordinary subtractions?

THE SILHOUETTE

The grave's incredible silhouette
Falls through the iron work of days,
Colossus, booted in regret,
Toppling forever in the shade.

Unquarried ebony of mind
Disqualifies the flower of ease,
But the beginning sprouts the end
Straight at our generation's eyes.

Across the luminous frame of time,
Barrage of dust, the shadow falls,
And leaves about the indelible tomb
To chide the bosoms of the hills.

Chromium-clean the cloudbanks lie
Racing the rooflines of the world;
In the geared grooves of nerves below
Atomic matter towers stalled.

With skylines in their teeth, the brave
Crawl from the cisterns of the wind,
And out of substance bleeds the shade
As though it were a wall of wound.

And civilization's painted frond
Darkens beneath a thunderhead:
The silhouette leans from beyond
Its age of doorways on our bread.

MAN IN HIS FATAL HUNGER

Man peers into the gulf of his large hand
And sees a storm of statues laboring there:
Before the darkening disk of distance stands
The ghastly jaguar combing his leprous hair:

Among the bubbling amber straw of stars
There glides, with planets shunting on its back,
An insect, vanishing through fragrant doors
While time is smoking sky above a shack:

And in the throes of a vast negligence
The strange hyena at the lighted glass
Foams at the tensile ligaments of sense
Its horrible laughter lashing at the grass:

Hyena, jaguar, insect—these draw breath
And balk the hero climbing into land:
Man in his fatal hunger knows no death
So deep as the abyss within his hand. . . .

THE BLOCK PARTY

I

The eyes like gimlet holes upon the dark
are widening inward, large as velvet moons,
remembering the dancing on the block,
the gaiety, the lanterns, the balloons—

how feet against the lights turned the huge spokes
of that slow wheel of darkness sparking stars
as the accelerated rim loosed flocks
of birds in walls of music past the doors. . . .

How the boys romped and all the dear girls sang,
and flowers drowsed upon the hair and wind:
ah, musical were jargon and harangue
and mandolins and candy of the mind!

And all the songs of nations gathered there,
merry-go-round around the captive birds:
no aeroplanes to gorge on flesh of air!
no radios to crop the stems of words!

O street roped off against all evil feet,
against the rumbling of the cobbled day,
here in your orange twilight, it was sweet,
here at the perfumed stairway, it was gay!

Young were the dewy lips of circumstance,
deep in that bower, that carillon of tongues:
so many hearts so happy all at once
shook the millennium through a sieve of wrongs!

II

The moons condense to pinholes at the stroke
of memory's gong on gates with death's-heads wrought:
and thirty years, a feather's height of smoke,
bloom for a moment at the focused thought.

The bombing surf of all our hidden tears
tilted its sunless combers on our hair,
and when we dared lift hearts again, the years
were clinker teeth, in armed formations there.

Alas, the aggregate heroic limbs,
a slimy mass of eyes, turned sky to stone:
now in our terminal the foreign hymns
warm their chilled fingers at the kindling bone.

There's fighting on the block, eastwest, northsouth,
it's shambles in the precinct of the dead:
the spongy clouds curl from the upturned mouth
toward seas of harpies pulsing overhead. . . .

A 1940 VACATION

(MacDowell Colony, Peterborough, N. H.)

Through my open door I saw the green field of June shining
Within a ring of trees resisting a great untiring wind:
And all the day that wind of poets washed the body of thought
And toppled towers of leaves, the buckling crags of green,
Or ploughed onward through armies of enormous whispers
With the rustling sound of all the dresses of history;
Then a tidal wave of trees stood up on the field's edge,
Lifted its paws of huge breakers and roared its verities
To my mind that sat looking from the very ledge of my eye.

But I remembered—remembered the snow in the mail-box,
The panic in the twenties and the run on the Lord's prayer,
The man crushed against the elevated pillar by a skidding car,—
I remembered the Negro hovel in the shadow of the White House,
And the milkman leaving the milk on the suicide's doorstep.

Through the wide-open environs of a personal vacation
Time poured endless confetti of creaky hinges of birdsound:
And the magnificent cold water of New Hampshire burned
Its quicksilver solder, a knife of ice, through my veins
Until the brain became a glittering peacock's-tail of streams:
And all those long days long my mind sang in poems,
And nature laid out the miles of damask, sunset upon sunset,
Or filled the air with tons of the thick lace of rain,
Or sat on tall dark stools of clouds on amber afternoons
Dangling the limbs of giant cogitations at the windows,
While the sky of democracy, blue and bland, hung on.

But I had heard of the arrow in the eye of Harold, last Saxon,
Of the Spartan boy with the hidden airplane gnawing his vitals,
Of the millennium of the Aryans foaming at spigots of beer,
Of the refugees praying to the hills of lead in the sky—
But I remembered—remembered the blackened munition workers
Sweating at midnight to blow the morning from babies' brains.

JEREMIAD: XIV

Ah, language like a landslide invades the chairs,
The tables, the furniture, the midnight layout,
And the statue on the estate leaps down the stairs,
The telephones ring, the atoms are burning,
The verbs are running, the skylines are churning,
And the sirens hunt down the ultimate blackout:

The eyeline is giving where the clouds are heaving
And the winds are blowing the landscapes shut,
The leaves are lugging the trees unmoving,
But man's minnow-dream escapes the snaring
By the nightlight of doubt—and matter is wearing
Down, down, down to its bones of light.

And even these bones fracture in the brain,
The splinters are gleaming between the phrases:
The rain's harp playing over meadows of grain
Sprinkles the darkness with lightning beginnings,
But the doubtful knowledge, the forsaken winnings
Take from the archives the sense of oasis.

The archives ring with the silence when a coin
Of the sun is spun from the wrist of horizon:
And doors of midnight open at the groin
And the heads come out to see through the shutters
The enormous seraph writhing in the gutter,
The engine of invasion on the lawn of reason.

Let the carpers take care, let the eaters stop,
For the elements lean on their crumbling elbows,
The fissures of lies like a chopper shall lop
The smirk from their wisdom, kings from the coins,
The grisly generations from their pampered loins,
And tradition from the lips of all good fellows.

Let the owners disown, let the hoarders hide,
For the golden calf is a wooden horse,
Where claws of reckoning in the millions abide,
And soon they shall swarm on townclock and future,
On the shades of ideals and the tombs of whores,
On the tons of myth in the nerve stream of nature.

ON THE SUDDEN DEATH
OF A YOUNG ACQUAINTANCE

Friend, when I think of your delicate feminine face
And of your little hopes common as hearing or seeing,
How singlehanded you moved the massive stone of space
To find a cranny for the flower from the soil of your being,

And how now you manage to keep open in the universe
Under all-time strain that lighted crack in the reckoning
I am haunted by your grimace O steadily getting worse
Awaiting the vast glad look that reduces everything.

For long I thought you another human being in doubt,
One of the millions ordinary as daylight is everywhere,
One of those usual people that one meets with all about—
Now I see you were capable of decision and despair.

Forgive me if my heart cringes with those who die,
Forgive me, friend, when even in thought I cannot be brave
Who think of your clear face agonized under tons of sky
Hourly growing more haggard from the weight of the grave.

III THE GLASS CASE OF THE RIVER

THE GLASS CASE OF THE RIVER

Down the far reaches of the hollow dimension of the air,
Deep on the river, a boat like a gesture of silence moves:
The shoreline nerve of my unhappiness is honed thin
On the quicksilver water's perilous pounding of space.
With the multitudes heavy on my back, I front this hour,
Heartbreak storming back and forth through my senses.
The voluminous atmosphere booms by, important with the century,
While the sky slaps the river a million invisible times:
And I think of my years that fell down the stairs one day,
How the grinding stairs became locked in space, how I rose
With a crippled past, leaning a crazy pattern on the wind,
Like a brain alone, in a turret of bone, in the wind. . . .

Down the stone walk, through the wet marble of my reverie, comes
The ice cream man with his grocery face and shuffle of fate,
With his palatial perambulator, cracker jack, celluloid colors;
He shall inherit no biographer and very little of the earth,
But he is six miles tall down the angel's land of the children
Who, before your very eyes, behold! are deep in their past.
The park inhales mothers, servants, children, unemployed,
Exhales an household hour of near-by fashionable apartments:
The little boy at the fountain, shadowed by a cliff of nurse,
Like a dewdrop of flesh on the whitened brow of the afternoon
Yells as he falls through the moment hairy with eyebrow:
Alongside the glass case of the river, the park life moves on
Revealing again the silver heartbreak, leaving me stranded,
Crying for a chance in the world and a place,
A chance that is given with grace,
And a niche in the music of the race.

The competent sea gulls jockey for position in immensity,
They spin and toil in the air for little wet fish of the sea;
Now farewell wings wave from the clothesline of contemplation,
Now they are inkspots on cloth clouds, now holes in snow fields,
Now they battle with a vision propounding out of the waters,
And now are utterly undisturbed by the rumbling out of nowhere.
An airplane rolls the glint of the future from its wings, falls
Without acceleration across the sky, and buries itself
In a cloud of buildings that immediately composes the scene:
You will find my body, glazed with thought, on the stone bench,
With the falling moments scrambling through the five open senses:
I am alone, I am alone, I am alone,
A foghorn is whistling in my bone,
I float on a nightmare undertone.

Some day that undertone will invade the rarefied air
Of the skull, and make a job of it, and break the glass case
Of the river, and all these bridges painted in rich moth ink,
These red clay hills on the barges, the story-book lighthouse,
These golden eagles on the black boats, these modern myths,
This enormous dentist apparatus of the navigation companies
For mysterious feats of daring down ravines of daily bread,
These towboats, motorboats, all the harbor life shall spill
Out among these towers with the sound of exploding eardrums:
Then the housetops of foreign travel shall clatter in my brain—
The niche of music shall leap from the church of sorrow in vain
Like a finger of anger pursuing the godhead in flight
Where sings time, down instantaneous chutes of light.

MORNING OVER THE 20th CENTURY

Deep in the fog of multitudes honeycombing history,
Below the dance of the dimensions in mirrored sleep,
These familiar noises cut at my cardboard hour:
A train pulls into a spiral of dark sounds;
A milkman shakes the low bells of milk bottles
In the iron baskets of our civilization;
The horse's hoofs whip up the wagon wheels;
A cough reaches out an arm for an alarm clock;
A small dog's bark runs after a truck's sound
But makes no progress on the icy ground.
On my blood-and-bone balcony poised perilously
Over the morning canyons of the present tense
I arise to view the times I have awakened in:
Europe spreads helpless hands called newspapers
And leans against the horizon of a bleak intent;
A dictator is eating the apple in our garden
And war studies the scarred face of geography
Behind the Stonehenge framework letting in myths:
With distance stuck in its throat, a radio mutters;
The world's philosophies clack, like loose shutters.
This is the shadow from under steel lids of sunlight
That watches me dressing brightly in consciousness:
I hear an early morning whistle hang a blue icicle
Upon the lintel of my personal class struggle.
I must hasten to the heaven inhabited by breakfast
Where lunchrooms lurch forward on rolling plates
And coffee swings brown flowers through the senses—
For I am a citizen of the three divided tenses
And know a new day threatens to invade the sill
With all the past an unanswered problem still.

THE CHILDREN'S PLAYGROUND

This is the children's playground, the home of the inner eye,
Surrounded by the fences and benches against the unbridled dark,
Where the prodigious exuberance of the miniature human beings
Tests the chutes of gravitation, seventeen trees from the zoo.

This is the place where the adults are grotesquely overgrown,
Where other children's parents are statues out of their niches,
Where the tree of plurals grows, where time is over forever,
A sea of all directions for the wayward paddling of childhood.

This is the children's playground, the tenderest part of the park,
Where home buzzes behind a bush and nurse is a hillside of *don'ts*
Where every pigeon rolls along like a slowly stopping ball
And glittering birds fall from the hairy lips of fountains.

The squirrels adorn the trees with the scrolls of their tails,
And sparrows, those crumbs of birds, dart for their dots of bread;
The buildings stand in a crowded parade to see above each other,
The ambush of the everywhere is crowded with elbows, hats and toes.

With daylight, a common denominator, entering everything easily
The cars the day long on the streets play games of north-&-south,
The grown-up people sit all alone in the middle of their shops,
But this is the children's playground, seventeen aeons from lunch.

SHOPPING FOR MEAT IN WINTER

What lewd, naked and revolting shape is this?
A frozen oxtail in the butcher's shop
Long and lifeless upon the huge block of wood
On which the ogre's axe begins *chop chop*.

The sun like incense fumes on the smoky glass,
The street frets with people, the winter wind
Throws knives, prices dangle from shoppers' mouths
While the grim vegetables, on parade, bring to mind

The great countryside bathed in golden sleep,
The trees, the bees, the soft peace everywhere—
I think of the cow's tail, how all summer long
It beat the shapes of harps into the air.

THE PRAYING MANTIS
VISITS A PENTHOUSE

The praying Mantis with its length of straw
Out of the nowhere's forehead born full armed
Engages the century at my terrace door.
Focused at inches the dinosaur insect sends
Broadsides of epic stillness at my eye,
Above the deafening projects of the age.
My love, who fears the thunder of its poise,
Has seen it and cries out. The clouds like curls
Fall in my faith as I seize a stick to stop
This Martian raid distilled to a straw with legs,
To wisps of prowess. Bristling with motionlessness
The Mantis prays to the Stick twice armed with Man.

I strike, the stick whistles, shearing off two legs
Which run off by themselves beneath some boards.
The Mantis spreads out tints of batlike wing,
The many colored pennants of its blood,
And hugs my weapon; the frantic greens come out,
The reds and yellows blurt out from the straw,
All sinews doubtless screaming insect death.
Against the railing's edge I knock the stick
Sending that gay mad body into the gulf.
Such noisy trappings in defeat wake doubts.
I search my mind for possible wounds and feel
The victim's body heavy on the victor's heart.

ON THE COUCH

In a shack in the summer woods, 1943

To see my coat hanging there limp as a scarecrow's
On the back of the chair in the corner of the room,
Its agonized inertness eloquent of past motion,
Its very shapelessness fugitive of the body's form—

To see myself stretched out so like a road from my chin
In the exhausting lifetime journey from here to there,
To see the trees bend in at the windows as if measuring
The distance from the thought to the step in the air,

Who would dream that events like a storm are raging,
A cloudburst of jungles, and snarl up the inner eye,
That man is the animal caught in his own barrage
In a plague of grasshopper gadgets out of the blue sky?

And treetrunks pour backward fast on my right and left,
As my profile plunges forward, my fate is out gunning,
The black branches of leaves rush over my shoulders
Crashing, as I lie here, stretched out, running, running.

LITTLE STEAMBOAT

The harbor wears a look of space
But hides its foggy fists:
The little steamboat's sudden face
Comes dawning through the mists.

It stares at clouds whose charging bulls
Are roaming china skies:
On plates of blue, lie black sea gulls,
And steel pearls are their eyes.

The little steamboat, like a dream
Of distance through a spinet,
Sails up the tightrope of a gleam,
The skyline of a minute.

She comes from thirteen wicked coasts,
Five-cornered is her heaven,
And every man aboard her boasts
The sins that number seven.

And so she sports and snorts in rhyme
And spits at lolling lands
And beats the thin, tin sides of time
With hot and foggy hands.

THE HORSE OF ACCIDENT

The Horse of Accident was sitting next to me
And looking on at life with his prodigious horse face:
Beside me in the bus but freezing my right side
There sat this fellow passenger from senseless space.

How did he get into this modern modern bus
This man with veritable mane and fierce face of horse?
Out of his collar burst the bestial scorched neck,
And there he sat beside me, breathing snow or worse.

I saw those huge lewd eyes hung out upon the aisle,
Bloodshot, yes, and beastshot, they congealed the air:
I scurried from the corner of my eye into myself,
Looked at the street, the commonplace still crawling there.

I saw the New York traffic, the storefronts stolling by,
The cars and taxis manned by men in day's sweet light
And buildings stacked against the overtures of thought,
But that Presence crackled like a glacier on my right.

And I was cornered in a moment out of time
Between the moving tide and the horror by my side;
The other passengers showed unconcerned blank backs
And life was down to knees of rubber through that ride.

But how the knowledge came to me I do not know:
It was not Centaur, Houyhnhnm nor progeny of both,
But the clear sheer head of the damned long ago
Rearing as through a manhole the fury of its sloth.

LINES AT NIGHT

Here in the midnight in the desert of a pause
The lamp's light threatens to be gay forever,
Unblinking joy rinsing the permanent air
Long after the hands that woke it sleep in distance;
I see the bookcase standing up, rich like a tiger
Long after the authors have staggered into time.

The very paint upon my walls is an extension
Of people who have somewhere somehow planned,
Persisted in a nonsense till it reaches here
And heaps invisible implications on my senses;
The newspaper lies on the couch, blackly headlined
With chronic drama, fallen columns of type,
With here and there a picture, recipes, maps,
The price of sugar, a corrupt thoroughness of detail
Triggered in case I grow curious late at night.

I am served by an obsequious civilization
They say is rotting (O lively senility!)
Breathing its great care carefully drained of love;—
I am impressed. The presences of these things
Like blown-out candles beleaguer a self involved
And truth on its half-wings beats about in the room.

THINKING IN THE MIDNIGHT

Thinking in the midnight of my dread and need,
The room like a nervous birdcage around my head,
And far off the war breathing live hills of steel,
Tidal waves tossing beneath imagination's small bird,
Sitting here alone I ask, who is a friend, who?

No matter how I turn or where, the walls spin,
The world bobs, a birdcage in a strong wind,
The airshaft on the roof creaks, the cold leans
Its hairy invisibles into the room, and I behold
That horrifying breach, the economic face—

Unmitigated face eaten into by the greedy self,
The vitriol urge to power thrown straight
At the face terraced like lions in nature,
And the smoke of that burning so thick it hangs
Inert pillars of dust in the land of the heart.

Solid and black the smoke pouring from that face,
And deep the face, abyss that ate the small bird;
The light in my room, foiled, coils from the walls,
And Compassion amputated at its lifetime crawls
A hair's-breadth—horror is moss to the moment.

Who is not faced at last by the composite monster
Whose voice, gloved in the distant thunder of fate,
Orders extinguished the last bright drop of pity,
The hope thrown to the insatiable joke or jackal,
Obeisance of sense to the tyrannic interval?

Here is the horror that beggars the big war,
And to whom shall one turn in this nightmare time?
Oh, in a world so full of so many people, fine
Faces, hearts real as their blood, and children ir-
Revocably themselves, in a fierce universe where

One day washes out the seas and the continents
With its faith in extravagance, why is it so hard,
So hard, hard, to run to all of the people at once,
To cry out to them, to say, here I am, here am I,
I belong to you, amongst you, I am one of the human race?

79

IV BY FIAT OF ADORATION

BY FIAT OF ADORATION

This is what we really want
Who drink the kingdom of the heart
A toast to the imagination

She is flowering in a doorway
Eyes cheeks haze of hair
Stepping out of time into here

This is what we really have
Who see the one we adore becoming
The two that she is in the light

Ah God bounces all the waters
From hand to jubilant hand
He cannot contain Himself

But comes over into being
With benediction of painted cloud
The being whom to look at is to become

By fiat of adoration do we reach
The very muscle of miracle
The ease with which beauty is beauty

THE MIRAGE

I lived a life without love, and saw the being
I loved on every branch; then that bare tree
Stood up with all its branches up, a great harp
Growing straight out of the ground, and there I saw
A squadron of bright birds clothing the bare limbs;
The music notes sat on the harp; it was all love.

This was the heart inside the starved body;
Love grew images like cactus, and planted roses
On the walls of the mirage, and the garden grew
Shining with perfume and the senses dwindled to dew,
The century was rolled into one formation aloft,
A cloud, like St. Veronica's handkerchief of love.

There I saw the face of the one without whom
I lived, two soft jewels implanted in her face,
Her hair pouring around her face without sound,
And her love for me sprang on her skin like dew,
Pearl-grey as the flower of the brain she lay
Quivering on the soft cushion of the great day.

I heard a roar of buildings at my conscience,
I looked up and saw a wall of windows glowing,
And there my love leaned out of each window,
There she leaned out multiplied like heaven
In that vast wall of lights, every light her face,
Suns of a thousand mornings ranging on one day.

And all the machines were running, and yes, great
Was the sound of their running downward and down
Into the blind chutes of their rooted feet,
And all of the windows quivered with my many loves,
Like apples they fell off, at one windfall, all,
And I awoke on the starved pavements of no love.

THE ANSWER
USUALLY COMES IN WORDS

The answer usually comes in words, but this is a basket,
A man all covered in straw lying deep in the bulrushes,
And Pharaoh's daughter, her face a benign lamp of love,
Shines over him, surrounded by a province like a future.

The adult is fully armed, though embalmed in the sleep
Of his senses, the latest newborn bulging from the instant;
The servants must ask no questions, the king never know,
A new source has fallen on the grounds of our problems.

Come, are you strong enough to walk, to talk, to climb
The giant beanstalk shining now with new manufacture?
A gulf with mossy sides is the pride of our public park,
Faraway snow covers the pavements that run to horizons.

Pharaoh's soldiery is playing checkers in the glassgold
Greenhouses, and Pharaoh's daughter is wearing drugged bees
In her hair, and honey flows like a river beside the taxes,
The whole world will wait until you die ere it buries you.

Get up and out, my man, the day is bursting with moments,
The attendants have kitchens stored up in the distance,
The river weaves in among the bulrushes its minnows of music
To charm the fountain of halfsouls gathering within you.

And Pharaoh's soft daughter walking like a pair of seraphs
Topped by the bounty of her face, a nosegay of dazzles,

Shall lead you by the hand to the waterfall's bright wall,
Into her chambered twilight papered with the real birds—

Into her secret chamber where her emotions like birds
Shall fly around her probable heart in a ring of parables,
You shall pick from her halo a favored one with your finger,
And two birds will fly straight into your eyes to find you.

Rise from the basket in the bulrushes for time is shining
Like a kingdom with lights, and in time you shall be king,
Your love wear the northern lights' ceremony like a crown;
Rise, my good man, from your bed of straws in the wind.

ON MEETING A STRANGER
IN A BOOKSHOP

We stand talking in the cave whose walls are
The colors—like rock under a veil of nettles—
Of the books' backs embedded as if forever;
The writing on the wall is overweening with titles.

I talk to you, the bare light burns above
Like the apple of Eden pulsating its sparks,
And in this small space we sail as in a closed
Balloon through the vast astronomical works.

I tell you the most intimate thing I am,
My name, and yours floats out to me, creeps
Into ears' trumpets, folds itself around my brain:
Holding hands thus we sail off into the deeps.

We sail off and are the angels again and again
Affirming the sensational power of a thought;
We leap down a star to the land of shouldn't,
Or stand looking wanly into the window of ought.

The world (it's a world!) leans heavily outside
Its breathing against the walls of the cave;
Strangely, we are flying both inside and outside,
We blow to cool off a Venus rising on a wave.

Our wings are bright doubts hoisting at our backs
With an elaborateness that embarrasses the dragon

Of gravitation who looks up with large sweet orbs
Of chagrin and churns up conventions in his wagon.

We have stepped out with the buoyant daring step
Of a rainbow on its seven-league binge of color;
Chips of philosophy and verse, platitudes' powder,
Star-pollen, too, softly cling to our shoulders.

We come then to ten black birds facing each other
Like fingers of the hands under a tree's bent back
And busily lacing the twigs of the long boot—
Good-bye, we say, to the problem there in its track.

Finally like children we have run out of ourselves.
I put on my coat and you pretend to be hurried.
We let go our clinging eyes and the cave caves in:
The books tumble on our heads and we are buried.

SPRING

The bird that flies to climates crisper
Over its feathers wears feathers of sound
Protecting itself in a coat of whispers
Against the silence that stones the ground.

In the long miles between song and hearer
Where the distance's bones lie disinterred
I now overhear as the wings come nearer
The whispers of God instructing the bird,—

And see Him put out the branch of a finger
Where the bird sits down and begins its cheers;
The buds push out to look at the singer,
The blades of grass stand up all ears.

O truly now, it is gayer and warmer,
Tomorrow's the only dark bush on the land
And full of its doubts, but God the performer
Is walking about with the bird in His hand.

THE SERAPHS

Branches whose buds are birds
Lean in through frames of song:
Man's house is full of words
And every word a tongue.

At doors that cannot close
And shutters that fall slack
The bursting music blows
Its storm through every crack.

The fireplace eyes the room
And lifts the flames that drowsed
To guide through gulfs of gloom
The seraphs now aroused.

Their eyes are steep and wild
With dews of deep desire:
Upon the sills are piled
The hissing hills of fire.

The landscape packs its tongues
Of distance through the door:
A million demon prongs
From sundown's ingot pour.

Unleashed are lightning wrists
And all the wings that browsed
In flocks upon their breasts—
The seraphs are aroused!

JUDAS

When first he saw the savage lilies in the meadow
They broke a great sheet of silver on his forehead,
Their purity crackled and his heart grew frightened,
His inner eye trembled by his outer heightened,
Never knowing whether to be cringing or demanding
He became the high priest of all misunderstanding.

He made his senses his law and knew no other,
And always there was the shadow of his brother
Cleaving the rich sunlight into toppling flowers,
The domain of his brow darkened and his soul soured;
Enemies kept growing on trees crowding the branches,
A cloud of arms reaching for his morning's chances.

The field of lilies glittered in the light of honor
Cool among the mountains, but steadily came rumors,
He continued hearing calumnies against his having,
Tall talk of all kinds of giving and of loving;
In time he trafficked between Susanna and the elders
And became the outsider with the uneven shoulders.

Born with the forever on the night of the Supper
A wall of angels sang he was to live and suffer;
Now his church has grown gigantic under the bushel
Sending beacons of blasphemy on the individual;
O but he bore witness that every man of ill will is
Crazed by a glimpse of the sea of silver lilies.

THE LAST SUPPER

I

Apostles of the hidden sun
Are come unto the room of breath
Hung with the banging blinds of death,
The body twelve, the spirit one,
Far as the eye, in earth arrayed,
The night shining, the supper laid.

II

The wine shone on the table that evening of history
Like an enormous ruby in the bauble and mystery.

In the glowing walls of the flickering decanter
There moved His face as at the world's center.

The hands of Judas showed up red and hurried
And the light hit them so, like a cross carried.

The faces of the others were there and moving
In the crystal of the dome, swiftly hovering.

The saints, under a lens, shrunken to pigmies,
Gesticulated in birds or in colored enigmas.

Outside there was a storm, the sound of temblors,
The blood bubbled and sprang into the tumblers.

When the morning came like a white wall of stone,
The day lay in the glass and the blood was gone.

CHANT

As God claps hands of time and space
The leaves in millions fall in place
The land becomes by flowers refined
A shade around the flame of mind
And lovers figure in the park
And gravestones settle in the dark
But kingdom go or kingdom come
Rejoicing is where we are from

The sun burns free of might and main
In that far realm beyond the rain
But like a hand in agony bound
The root unclenches in the ground
And millions catch the sun's great eye
And millions hold with roots to die
But kingdom womb or kingdom tomb
Rejoicing is where we are from

The midnight long the sharp stars put
Their blistered lips against our thought
The loving profile of that sleep
Talks with a voice a lifetime deep
And yet the morning on our eyes
Lays the twin flower of the skies
As from a festival we come
Rejoicing is where are from

Though paradoxes live in words
And facts stampede in frightened herds

A glory beats its feathery shades
Like wings behind our shoulder blades
And lifts us swiftly on the earth
As if still on our way from birth
O now until millennium
Rejoicing is where we are from

THE FIRST BORN

The world was born ahead of me. O monstrous twin!
I put a bud forth beneath a bower full of things,
Branches, all elbows, but gestures ending in fruit;
Shadows of clouds tilting with shadows of leaves;
The whole world got here before me, a crowd.

I spend a lifetime panting, who have been
In a fearful race with the swift hand of God;
My eyes fly through the storm in my head;
Small are the shadows cast by feathers of sight;
The clouds with one dimension images brush the ground.

I cannot travel fast enough to catch the world
Successfully born first; the meadows run off with grass;
I close my eyes, the sun leaps beneath my thought
A fireball on the string of an idea, the fruit above
Swings, blossoms rain, the rain blossoms aloud.

It was a head-on collision of the atom with
The planet, a birth in the face of everything dying;
O garden, clasping a bud to your miles of bosom,
You are caught in the act of celebrating my coming:
A welcome so big it can never be worn out.

V   THE SEESAW

THE SEESAW

I   I sit on the surge called ten stories tall
My eye flattens to a floor, a wall,
Like any bird on the nest anywhere
I live in a constant nothing of air
Some forty years up and ten stories high
A hundred inventions ahead of the sky,
With a ladder of ancestors holding me up
Whose rungs into history mystery drop,
But here I am where faith's feathers fly
Like the child in the rhyme in the sky so high.

Over the plumes of your thoughts I see
Your tired heart resting beside a tree;
From the tenth platform of my tithe of time
I perceive you exhausted in your prime,
With heaven collaterally circling around
Your presence that holds the landscape down,
With birds disappearing in the sponge of leaves
And sundown painting your hopes in sheaves—
I speak into a tube for your distant ear,
You look up at me across the miles so clear.

Is it your look makes my room to descend
As though I were inside the shaft of the end?
The floorspace edges from under my feet
The breadth of a sword's edge of monstrous speed;
I grasp for the desperate point of a tear,
For the bend in space or the turn of the year,
But out of the thousands not the least star
Can keep me from falling too fast too far;
And suddenly there beneath your tree I lie
With you at the window ten stories so high.

II My face hung out its search in front of me,
    A mask to try the outer storm of space,
    Or net of form cast in the sea to be,
    To catch at things not safely in their place
    Out building coral pinnacles; on the fly
    When heaven was stretched on rocks of cloud I caught
    A tall star in the corner of my eye—
    Lassoed was I, prone on the floor of thought—

    Thrown, like the fisherman's wife who asked too much
    In wanting to be God; the lightning's hiss
    Foamed at the peak of earth, full height to touch
    And hope, but death-rayed down to an abyss,
    This now-deep nothingness on which we're curled.
    It is the stars that make a valley of the world.

III Divine seesaw! Rise in thine arc of higher!
    The valley of the grave holds up the stars.
    The hand on the big Dipper trembles, pours
    The fields of gold that roll out on the mire;
    And in those fields there boils another sun
    Stamping his weight until the night's stars drive
    My unlived ages to the land of none
    From which the sunflower shakes his flames alive—

    And fire breaks out in my friend's house of rules,
    The light in my neighbor's window burns my soul,
    My enemy falls heir to all of Christ's jewels,
    The loved one in the moving grave swings clear,
    The grave and window seesaw before the whole,
    The hill wears orbits of the dust and wind.
    O pivot's pressure at the heart, through you I hear
    The universe hallooing for an end.

99

EYE OF SLEEP

He lies asleep, his arms around this night,
Body, an eyelid, closed about his soul;
    The soul like to an eye
    Is wide awake as sky
And looks in all directions through the dark.

Then loosened heavens the gaze within engage,
The iris widens at the charge of goal;
    On rims where space is set,
    In clouds of time not yet,
As though sleep-walking, floats the globe of sight.

The lights turn gold the massed fogbanks of age
Retreating from the eye of wisdom's birth;
    In posture of the dance
    The body holds its trance
Head in the sand, breath-deep in sleeping earth.

O eye enlarged until you take in God,
You have your vision of the great redoubt—
    Contract into the man
    As swiftly as you can,
Fall not asleep as morning comes without.

UPON FINDING A DEAD INSECT
IN THE LEAVES OF A BOOK

In what deep languorous summer night
Peopled by the wind of things in flight
Above the flowers asleep like seed
Did you go searching for something to read?
Your tiny blond wings a tawny dust
You blur all sense with your tinge of quest,
For what you wanted and who you were
Have joined the revels of flake and star.

Did you explore at a lamplit head,
A planet lost in a nebula of bread,
Nor see that giant of body move
To cast a sweeping shadow on love?
Was there a falling wall of light
On which at the end you hastened to write
An illumined postscript to the dark
Reducing your meaning to a final mark?

Or were you the insects' advance patrol
Charged to decipher the human soul?
Did you radio your armies to hide
As at the borders of the mind you died?
Caught by a squadron of words you arrive
(An onion in a bag is more alive);
And yet there gleams in your delicate gauze
As you lie still the light of your cause.

These words in barracks around your grave
The eloquence of your dying crave;
Could they speak through your voice of death
As you through the archives of man's breath
They would proclaim the news you sent
Between the lines as the world's event,
And reach whatever ears may be
Beyond the ring of mortality.

MAN WITH KEYS

A man with his pockets full of keys
Trots mountains of moments down the street:
(Man's pockets bulge with finalities):
Where is he running in such a heat?
The houses like walls of soldiers stand,
Their glassy windows bristle now:
The sound of keys is beating the land,
Metallic surf against man's brow.
The sunset reddens at the sound
And calculates the sum of schemes:
Chump-chump in pockets' deep expound,
The keys have voices in man's dreams.
A man is running belled with keys,
The mice of time are wreathed in smiles:
The wrinkled lead and gold of seas
In tumbling cherubs chase the miles.
Windows fill up with teeth of skies
The keys are brushing buildings' lips:
A man is busy running from lies
The keys agog upon his hips!
Stop, my bad man, your aimless quest,
Houses are keyholes, don't you see?
The thieves of haste alone infest
The archives of such property.
Go turn your pockets inside out,
Shake out the dies of your distrust,
And try the ringed keys of your doubt—
Unlock, unlock, unlock the dust.

103

BALLAD OF THE LOSER

I had lost in the game of chance
    The child's and the mother's food,
When I left the dice in their dance
    And stumbled into the wood.

My head was numb with the wine
    My feet were dazed with the loss;
Naught but my body was mine
    And I lay down in the moss.

The thunder reared in a cloud
    A fury of overhead;
I was deep in the darkness, bowed
    By the fate that ate my bread.

It is said in the good old book
    Rewards are on every tree,
But the tree under which I shook
    Was full of tears like the sea.

My body bent to those blows,
    My spirit wilted in the flood,
I had not a thing more to lose
    Who had lost the sense of good.

I had lost in the game, was beaten,
    But the storm piled cloud on cloud.
O senseless heaven, to threaten
    Long after your victim is cowed!

MILK AT THE BOTTOM OF THE SEA

In the bowl of buildings *alias* the back yard
The milk of snow endlessly pours, but the bowl never
Fills. The century's live inhabitant caught behind
The window pane watches the single rakish tree
Blaze forth in ponderously immaculate italics.
The snowflakes pour everywhere in a panic, dizzyingly,
Or whirl to re-organize in the mid-air and float
Undecided; the sky tilts its ominous mountain, insuring
Another waterfall of snowflakes with all feathery speed.
Such activity should be noisy, a school's-out! of sounds,
But the silence is reverberating on the window glass
Exploring the deep-sea life of waywardness.

I am a traveller in the middle of the winter
In a wood-and-glass ship on the deeps of the age.
From peril's hold I watch the white germs from heaven
And blithe nothingness, the delicate roe of purity
Splurging to fill the air with their multipleness,
Making not even the sound of rain against rock.
I am an eye, I know, frozen in an undersea façade,
And have lost my hearing in such fantastic depths
Where the pressures cave in the senses, but still
My eye kindles to all this whiteness bearing down
In a dance of spiritual blindspots on our town.

In the end the wandering snowflakes are driven
Together, foam fat in the bottom of time, and I
Assuage through the mouth of the mind my entity;
The army of my veins, blood-drops, pores, thoughts

Crowds to my bones in one supreme act of gravity,
Closer than earth to a hill, than leaves to a tree,
Till I am the very body of oneness and cannot go
Pure, cold, diffuse and wayward like the snow.

THE PATTERN

The moment's lastingness hangs a pattern of leaves
Dealing in the swift cards of light and shade;
This dazzling sleight of time shuffling the blood
Casts a sea of leopards' spots upon the road.

The wanderer pauses in the dominion between thieves
Shielding his mind against the blindspot's storm.
The pattern keeps a changeling eye on form
And pokes in the joker dark, dark is the norm.

Rich with never, a wilderness of no in hand,
The moment stays canonized overhead just so long
As the wanderer is in the woods of right and wrong,
His cave of face clapped round a cowering tongue.

But when he leaves a loser the table and the land
The leaves above him crane from napes of stemlessness,
The pattern showers its flowers of more on less,
And it is no no no all the way to the border of yes.

ŒDIPUS

I am haunted by the face of the Mater,
The Mona Lisa smile of the heavens,
Dimpling at the corners of the lips with the sun
And the moon, the curve of all cradles between,
With the teeth in hiding, dark and waiting,
Savage, white wolves in the black air,
The face steps back in time, dancing.

Focused at the shuddering lifetime
The picture bounces like a great balloon
On the pearly grasses of morning
And the trees walk through the bubble of space
Dancing, their skirts above their heads,
With sounds excaping from the inner mind,
Bird-bodies of gleam, airbubbles gurgling up.

The portrait smiles through the shimmering heat,
A rending is heard in the early frame,
The house is telescoped through its largest window,
The walls glass, the glass curved, everything dances,
Pictures on the scarf waving in the bull's eye,
The goaded fury raises the slow dust of sleep,
A dance to the death of death.

I am haunted by the vast smile of everything
That slipped out of the gilt frame holding
The sun for a nightlight, as the bubble
Turns over its gold corpse, marine,

And all the fish duelling forever beneath time,
Scarves in shreds, rainbows in beds,
Secret lights on the horns of the dilemma.

DAWN OF ALWAYS

The young face of the late day,
The sun a spangle in its eye,
Stares, blue sky through a veil of twigs,
Seeing how the old add wine to their blood.

A city of pores, the tree breathes,
Emitting leopard's spots and slim birds,
With contrivances for clouds about.
Time gets old, old, but not the mind.

The mountain is dark and brown and spreads,
The sand, poured out, races the sea,
The edifice leans, wounded with windows.
But the late day wears a young face,

Blessed with eyes, gifted with hands.
History is powdered to a breeze,
Nothing is left but the fragrance,
Nothing but the sense of beginnings.

I hear the limbs of the past are big.
Importance is a frightening thing.
If the birds knew they wouldn't sing,
They sing, and the coming of today's day

In stars is signalled, winkings in the face
Of light's blizzard where the air lies
In mountains brushed by our eyelashes.
The heart is a snowflake on the cheek of space.

The old things lie the worst, their say
Deafens from tulips' crazed trumpets—
Their gay guns cough blood on the land,
But Gabriel's horn blows in the veins

The pæan of the dawn of Always at the
Pitch of now, and is of the bone of birth.
The rooster crows forever upon the earth
The sound of dreams widening into day.

III

THE HUNTER

The lord of the yeas and the nays
Was hunting through his days,
When he came upon a tree
In the middle road of Be,
Boldly in the centre it grew,
It said to the lord, you, too.

Said the lord of the yeas and the nays,
I am the one for three ways,
To my left the yeas, to the right
The nays are the stays of my might,
But I shall look in this tree
That dares the middle of Be.

He climbed till he reached the leaves,
That grew on the boughs in sheaves,
He searched through the mid-air bushes
Where the wind is sieved for thrushes,
But round the trunk they came
The hounds of ice and flame.

And baying loud their impatience
They shook the roots of the distance,
The leaves fell off on their haunches,
And tangled in a cage of branches,
A quarry of the yea and the nay,
Was the lord of the middle way.

THE HUB

The lights along the shore at night
Make spokes of flame upon the sea;
These twinkling shafts radiate
From where I stand, the hub of me.

Imagination the long rim
So swiftly treads a road of stars
The wheel kicks up the years in hills,
The dust of peace, the drift of wars.

The spokes now probe around for God
And in that nest of search I lie
Close to the miracle of the man
Who walked the waters and the sky.

THE BORROWER OF SALT

The man who saw the light hanging on the tall end
Of the road thought it was a lantern on the distant wall
Of the mysterious neighbor, so he said, friend, friend,
I am coming out to borrow some of the savor of your salt.

Wherewith he started running toward the light that hung
In the neighbor's window, and as he kept going the light
Danced, saying with a mocking step, isn't it wrong
That I dance in my glory while you walk in the night?

Yes, said the man, it is wrong, and what is worse
The wind is getting bad, the mud thicker, the road
Harder to follow and I move as slowly as a hearse,
In fact I feel as if my body were turning into the load.

The gleam tittered like a light on the end of a spar
But the man was up to his knees in road as if roots
Sprouted from his feet; alas, said the man, it is too hard,
Those who would walk in great men's tracks must wear boots.

He turned around and the wind opened spigots of swift air
On his head, up his thighs he felt the earth's lips creep,
And lo, the light gleamed spiritedly from his own fair
Housetop, but he couldn't move, the track was so deep.

THE BALI STONE BICYCLE

Let us go riding
On the Bali stone bicycle,
Flowers at the wheels
Silently gliding,
The stone bell peals,
The eyesight reels,
As in the heart gathers
A huge stone icicle.

Let us go riding
On the Bali stone bicycle,
Along the great wall
Covered with writing,
Time enough to fall
When the end comes to all
And the heart itself drops
Like a huge stone icicle.

Let us go riding
On the Bali stone bicycle.
Stone are the wheels,
Stone are the flowers,
Stone are the steels,
The petals and pedals are stone,
And the stone is crawling
Over the heart in one—
O murderous Medusa,
What have you done?

THE LADY WITH THE GLASS TORSO

The lady with the glass torso
And the wooden face of nowhere
Is sitting in the parlor
Between the statues and the mohair.

Bound by the strands of moment
Her heart is a package of words:
Touch her skin with your finger—
It parts like a floor of birds.

If you are gaunt from wanting
If walls close in on your bed,
A pillow made of wind sound
She shall stuff beneath your head.

Like diamond cutting glass
Desire shall cut your reason,
And all the windows fall out
On the scene of your liaison.

Between the banks of her lips
Shall stream the jewelled blood:
Upon the maidenhair meanwhile
Lies the flower of innerhood.

The lady with the glass torso
And furs of cloud on her shoulders
Shall publicly burn your mind
In the street aloud with elders.

Then inhale the fumes of oblivion
And break your heart in the wine,
Your actions all are courtiers
And in time shall make her thine.

Grow your eyes on her ringlets,
Tighten the chords of your veins,
And think of her in hosannas
When the sky looms through your chains.

The lady with the glass torso
And the wooden face of nowhere
Is waiting for you in the meadow
Between the stars and the snow there.

ALI BABA AND THE FORTY THIEVES

The invulnerable smile of the abstract
Is spread across the past,
A cobweb's pattern of acquiescence
Covering the Holes of Calcuttas;
Experience is a door in the ages
Formidable and delicately balanced,
As Ali, the ace Individual,
At the wall of the answers mutters.

Beside him lie the travelling bags,
Precarious pills and relationships,
The loot of the sleight-of-hand,
The sea of numbers and its froth;
He knows well that death's back tooth
Is sitting in the smirk of moment,
He hears how terrifying it is
Inside the aggregate mouth.

The slabs of quartered conscience
Hang on the tenterhook facts
While the silence is blaring around
The delicate entrails of brotherhood.
What demon on naked feet
Is whispering behind his shoulders
Advising on the job of landscaping
The lunar acoustics of the blood?

Beneath a wide sweep of grasses
Dotted with tombs of commandments

The I's ancestor and its progeny
Hear through the security of others
The thunder of the forty marauders.
The thieves tunneling toward Now
And all the aerials of his being
Tremble, remembering his brothers.

Ali is the man in the gulf
Mumbling the Sermon on the Mount
As the moths of remorse attack
The chance incandescent with heaven;
The horn of plenty on the wall
Bubbles with the trinkets of self
While from the far tenets of the era
The horsemen converge on the cavern.

Tapping the desperate make-believe
The Goliath eye of lament
Fumbles at the cleft in the age
For reality, boulder of despair;
Sesame! a wish fulfillment
Takes off on a runaway faith,
The door to freedom swings open,
His forehead is open on the air.

So the dark whisper, perception,
Goes through the rock's riddles,
Escapes to the tree's head-dress,
A metropolis of keyholes for eagles,
And Ali beholds the robbers there
The close-cropped napes of the years,
Stirrups of crusaders for tyranny,
Whispering fetlocks and silent bugles.

He watches the wrongful owners,
The brawn of evil in the sunlight,
The jewelled skulls of the rituals
Dancing at the leprous saddles,
The murderous courage of the knaves,
The originals of the womb's plurals,
The calloused fanatics bobbing
High on the sea of cradles.

Ali, dumpling thought hidden
In the tree's corrugated countenance,
Perspective of porous achievement,
Several leagues from wordsound,
Sees clouds of dust, bombs bursting
As if thrown at the heels of robbers,
While time and an airplane overhead
Skim the creamy miles of birdsound.

And as the plane roars along the edges
Egging on the sloth imagination
A lone horse cropping in the meadow
Lifts his tall tail a smack;
Ali descends to a present
Drained of the savor of complacence,
The peace of poverty vanished,
Riches, alas and alack.

This is the way he inherits
The forty enemies in the wind
Drilling now with their gimlet guilts
The walls beyond idea's range;
The tiger's eye at the front door

Is the same as at the back window,
Sleepless as the mushroom of wrong
Time is the jungle for revenge.

Pearl in the hippopotamus flesh
Glow-worm in the astronomical dark,
Ali lights up a palatial language
Forty floors in a circus of nerve-ends;
His fat musicians dandle all day
The amorphous routine interims
While viands vainly illuminate
Like candles the gloom of the servants.

But softly the pawing clouds touch
The asbestos eyelids on Baba
Cushioned in pillows of his wealth
Against the monopoly of crisis,
And he wakens to hear his slave,
Her radio voice nibbling the records,
How the future arrives in forty jars,
Each jar a sieve for his losses.

With his back against his possessions
On a day of great retreats,
He must face the tarantula growing
Its limbs in all corners of the cave,
The enemies that inhabited the wind
Are behind the navel of the absolute
Coiled in their fœtal postures
And armed to the flowers of the grave.

But light, says the slave girl, light
Burns the bigamy of the past tense,

The oil for the lamps of China
Shall cauterize the sperm of the strangers;
Like a camel panting at a needle eye
Ali raises his consummate anger
And stabs the hoodlum with seraph eyes
As the firedrill gong rings changes.

Song, says the slave, is a crown
For the bleeding brow at the climax,
The traitors to the peace are lying
On the back of resistance in a swoon;
Let us declare a jubilee, says Ali,
For the overplayed nervous system,
And discuss the problems of art
By the sterling light of the moon.

VI SEQUENCE & CONSEQUENCE

I THE WOODEN HORSE OF MYTH

The wooden horse of myth stands on the air
arching a traitorous neck on roofed mankind;
the clocks are eyes and wide with mock despair
hunting in sanguine skylines of the mind:
and cherubs' faces fluttering in position,
dolls tethered by the nerves behind the curtain
and soldiers draped about the foiled ignition
portend an end momentously uncertain.
Meanwhile the white-haired meadows of the sea
sing in the fixtures of the music box:
the crowning glory of the verb to be
marches its fields of fire among the rocks—
while tides of flowers topple from the blood
and horseless hills affirm their mountainhood.

II THE GAZE

The Everywhere's keen glance of innocence,
pretending history has never been,
with alps and orchards glittering through events,
takes charge of the results that drape the bone:
and dawn, a fire that burnt the past, now comes
with the vast brow, with large clean hands of winds,
and turns upon our rumors and our drums
the look that cauterizes all the wounds.
And while the soldiery of ignorance
drag smoking gunwheels up a sloped surmise,
and death from thickets of the present tense
aims airplanes at the grandeur in those eyes,
we feel it on us, though our days are halved,
that cloudless gaze in which we, too, are solved.

III MAN, WOMAN AND MOUNTAIN

The view lies like a windless veil collapsed
about explosive bones of distant earth:
the huge face wreathed in peaks of blazing teeth
is cropping trees behind a lake of maps.
In precincts lost to the hallooing eye
and torch of sunset lights the feather bed
and wakes the snake of sleep that aims its head
at nuggets thundering from thinning sky.
The deed is hammering at the rooms of mind
and calls the lovely woman at my side,
while Nature's awkward body tries to hide
O anywhere down reaches of the blind
The bulky mountain burrowing under rain
as Sex drags its glass corpse across the brain.

IV ALARM CLOCK IN THE CATSKILLS

The small persistent broken toothless clock
lies dying on the couch within the shack
that, too, lies slain upon the mountain rock
head down in reefs of twilight coughing back:
and still it hammers at the godhead air
so bludgeoned by the flowing sheets of stars:
the thin hands tear the tendons and the hair
of flesh sea-rinsed in sounds of shuffled doors.
Its minnow tongues peel tinfoil fortitudes
from walls of waves parked rearward in the blood:
it gasps through windows of our blue-veined moods
for ozone trickling down the bearded wood;
but casts against the barbed wire fence of light
the mountains hauled up from the infinite.

125

V MAN AND SQUIRREL

I walk through soggy hallways of the rain
and, past the bins of dried up daily bread,
meander to the pavements of the dead
with a glass squirrel chewing in my brain.
Its trembling paws adroitly turn and nurse
the fastened thought upon its screwed up features,
and with the long range eyes of silent creatures
it looks right through me at the universe.
There comes a sound of planets and of power
upon the sloped horizon's grassy eaves;
and I can stand, and will the brain endure
with stars stampeding down my final hour?
Of this, however, I am not quite sure.
My squirrel scurries up a cloud of leaves.

VI THE SPRITELY DEAD

There was a man within our tenement
who died upon a worn down step of day:
the wreath they hung upon the doorway meant
that there was nothing else for him to do.
But he was obstinate, he would not rest:
he dragged the flesh of silence everywhere
on crippled wings, and we would hear him whir
while on our memory's sill his eyes would roost.
We saw him wring his thoughts in deep despair
and stamp the color from our backyard scene:
careless, without his body, he would peer
to find out if we noticed his new sin.
He was afraid, afraid: he climbed our vines
and hid, on hands and knees, along our veins.

VII PORTRAIT OF REALITY

The ear, a fox, emerges from a cloud
of thunder perched above the universe:
the European headline in the crowd
crows copper morning from a hidden hearse.
Out of the flesh the jagged glass protrudes:
the sky is gleaming in the broken lenses
tapping the blood of giant platitudes:
scarred by hallucinations, roam three tenses.
Through mists of moss, the future's tom-toms come:
the past is dragging statues through the rain:
the present lives in spirals, hiding from
the starlight at the eyeballs of the brain:
the Buzzard's two great eyes of sun and moon
pop from the iron forehead of high noon.

VIII THE WARNING

The tiger deep in lilies and bleak rocks
moves with a special shadow down impartial sky:
his weighted paws flip mallets at the clocks,
freshness of death is dangling in his eye.
And recollections fall like mirrors from heaven:
immense, the wound of fear spills on the suns
where sound the lapping of the Deadly Seven,
the soft recoil of landscapes from the guns.
He who welds lilies to the tiger's flanks
and hangs black fists of cloud in caves of brain
and plants the planets on the moonlight's banks
trumpets through falling mirrors of the rain—
one sin has a steel skin and an icy tooth
and sinks its lightning in the fur of truth. . . .

IX PICTURE POSTCARD OF A ZOO

The zoo is full of cages and it lies
deep in the park but all around mankind:
the deadly bitterness of nature's lees
here gathers from foul pockets of the mind:
a temple to morbidity, it sprawls
through trees and down the vistas of the fictions:
giraffes live high in air, the bison drools;
the birds are screaming in a hundred factions.
The sky races above the tragedy:
the deer is nibbling at a crippled bird,
its fawn now stomps its hoof down on it hard;
next to the cage in which the yak will die
the boys are watching in a great to-do
the zebra's yardlong idling in the zoo.

X THE GREAT MARCH IS ON

The shoreline leaps beside the hurrying spars,
the ship is sailing on a sea of rain,
the sea is traveling in a land of stars,
the stars are vaulting onward into brain:
and the great march is on, and matter creaks,
and the vast corners are giving way fast:
the walls are shuddering back from gleaming peaks,
for we are breaking house with all the past.
It is no dream that tramples at the height:
the heartbeats swell to hills of ominous sound:
the quaint old landscape bends with myrmidons:
it is no go now just to stand our ground
in splendid failure while the changing suns
lash at our hollows with their feet of light.